Working Horses

Farm Horses

by Rachel Grack

Bullfrog Books

Ideas for Parents and Teachers

Bullfrog Books let children practice reading informational text at the earliest reading levels. Repetition, familiar words, and photo labels support early readers.

Before Reading

- Discuss the cover photo. What does it tell them?

- Look at the picture glossary together. Read and discuss the words.

Read the Book

- "Walk" through the book and look at the photos. Let the child ask questions. Point out the photo labels.

- Read the book to the child, or have him or her read independently.

After Reading

- Prompt the child to think more. Ask: Farm horses do many jobs that help farmers. Can you name other animals that help people do work?

Bullfrog Books are published by Jump!
5357 Penn Avenue South
Minneapolis, MN 55419
www.jumplibrary.com

Library of Congress Cataloging-in-Publication Data

Names: Koestler-Grack, Rachel A., 1973– author.
Title: Farm horses / by Rachel Grack.
Description: Minneapolis, MN: Jump!, Inc., [2024]
Series: Working horses | Includes index.
Audience: Ages 5–8
Identifiers: LCCN 2022049906 (print)
LCCN 2022049907 (ebook)
ISBN 9798885244930 (hardcover)
ISBN 9798885244947 (paperback)
ISBN 9798885244954 (ebook)
Subjects: LCSH: Horses—Juvenile literature.
Working animals—Juvenile literature
Classification: LCC SF302 .K635 2024 (print)
LCC SF302 (ebook)
DDC 636.1—dc23/eng/20221118
LC record available at https://lccn.loc.gov/2022049906
LC ebook record available at https://lccn.loc.gov/2022049907

Editor: Katie Chanez
Designer: Molly Ballanger

Photo Credits: Conny Sjostrom/Shutterstock, cover; Jim Parkin/Shutterstock, 1; Eric Isselee/Shutterstock, 3; Juniors Bildarchiv/SuperStock, 4; Becky Swora/Shutterstock, 5; Henk Osinga Photography/Shutterstock, 6–7; Pat & Chuck Blackley/Alamy, 8–9, 23tl; Jason Brubacher/Shutterstock, 10; Acerebel/iStock, 11; alexandrumagurean/iStock, 12–13, 23bm; Greg Kelton/Shutterstock, 14–15, 23tm, 23bl; oksana.perkins/Shutterstock, 16–17, 23br; nigel baker photography/Shutterstock, 18; intst/iStock, 19, 23tr; steverts/iStock, 20–21; Gregory Johnston/Shutterstock, 22tl; Dee Browning/Shutterstock, 22tm; Dennis W Donohue/Shutterstock, 22tr; David Gee 2/Alamy, 22bl; David Arment/iStock, 22bm; dhughes9/iStock, 22br; xpixel/Shutterstock, 24.

Printed in the United States of America at Corporate Graphics in North Mankato, Minnesota.

Table of Contents

Horses Help

The sun rises
on the farm.

It is time to work.

Farm horses will help.

shoulder

Farm horses are big and strong.

They have wide shoulders.

They do tough jobs.

They pull.

The farmer gives commands.
He tells the horses to walk.
Good job!

These horses work as a team.

team

This horse works alone.

plow

In spring, a horse pulls a plow.

The plow breaks up dirt.

The field is ready for seeds!

In fall, horses help with the harvest.

They pull a cart.

Their strong legs keep going!

sleigh

In winter, horses pull a sleigh.

Fun!

The horses are hungry after working.

They eat hay.

hay

The farmer grooms them.

19

It is time to rest.

Good job!

On the Job

Farm horses pull machines. Take a look at some of them!

vehicles
like wagons and sleighs carry plants or people

plows
break up dirt for planting seeds

planters
plant seeds

tedders
cut hay

rakes
collect hay into rows

balers
gather hay into bales

Picture Glossary

commands
Orders or
instructions.

field
A piece of open
land used for
growing crops.

grooms
Brushes or cleans
a horse.

harvest
The gathering of
crops from a field.

plow
A farm machine
that tills, or breaks
up, dirt.

sleigh
A vehicle pulled
through snow by
horses or other
animals.

Index

To Learn More

Finding more information is as easy as 1, 2, 3.

❶ Go to www.factsurfer.com

❷ Enter "farmhorses" into the search box.

❸ Choose your book to see a list of websites.